2429

The FIRST BOOK OF *Ancient Crete & Mycenae*

A seal stone from Vaphio.

The FIRST BOOK of

Ancient Crete
&
Mycenae

Charles Alexander Robinson, Jr

FRANKLIN WATTS, INC.
575 Lexington Avenue, New York 22

TO CELIA

© Copyright 1964 by Franklin Watts, Inc.
Library of Congress Catalog Card Number: 64-12120
Printed in the United States of America
by Polygraphic Company of America
1   2   3   4   5

Contents

GREECE IN THE BRONZE AGE

0 Miles 100

BOEOTIA, ATTICA, ARGOLIS

0 Miles 40

The Bronze Age

THE RUGGED ISLAND of Crete — 160 miles long and 36 miles wide, with Mount Ida in the center rising more than 8,000 feet — blocks off the Aegean Sea from the rest of the Mediterranean. To the south and east of the island lie Asia and Egypt, where, as early as 3000 B.C., there flourished a remarkable civilization. People lived in cities and had systems of government. They had learned to write, and knew something of science. Their art was extraordinary, and they had a body of literature. Moreover, they had established trade with other countries. All this had happened while Europe was still living in the Neolithic, or New Stone Age.

Situated as it is, Crete was the first part of Europe to be quickened by the advanced civilizations of Asia and Egypt. Trading ships from these countries brought not only goods but also new ideas to this island outpost of Europe. New experiences, new ideas waken men's minds and rouse them to greater efforts. The people on the island of Crete, stimulated by their contact with advanced civilization, began to develop a civilization of their own. This spread to such famous classical cities on the Greek mainland as Athens and Sparta, and finally from these cities to Rome. Rome, which conquered an empire, carried Greek civilization across Europe and to the British Isles. And so it was that a rocky island on the edge of the Aegean Sea is known today as the cradle of our own Western, or European civilization.

The great civilization which first developed around the Aegean Sea lasted from about 3000 B.C. to 1100 B.C. It is called the Bronze Age because at that time men learned to mix tin with copper to make bronze. As a material for making tools and weapons, bronze is far superior to stone, which had been used in Neolithic times. During the Bronze Age people began to live together in large towns. Big communities call for cooperation and organization, and this fact explains the rise of leaders and kings at this time.

The chief cities of the Bronze Age in Europe were Knossos, on the island of Crete, and Mycenae, on the Greek mainland. These two cities were rivals. Eventually Mycenae conquered Knossos; then, in 1200 B.C., it led the Greeks in a war against Troy, located in what is now Turkey. Troy, too, was part of the Bronze Age civilization, although it was an unimportant part.

The Bronze Age is the most romantic period in the entire inheritance of the Western world because, after it ended, the classical Greeks surrounded it with all sorts of tales. Yet, for three thousand years, all true knowledge of this period vanished from men's minds. The great cities of Knossos and Mycenae, the robber stronghold of Troy, existed only in myth and legend. Then, in the latter part of the nineteenth century and the beginning of the twentieth, these cities were literally dug up from the earth that had covered them for so many centuries, and the wonderful civilization of the Bronze Age leaped from legend to reality. This is how it happened.

A Man Who Believed A Myth

ABOUT THE BEGINNING of this century, when the Greek island of Crete belonged to Turkey, the Turkish Pasha, or governor, was passing the time of day with an Englishman at a coffeehouse in Herakleion, the island's biggest city and chief port. After a while the Turk turned to his companion and said, "You know, there is a fellow Englishman of yours poking around Knossos. He thinks there was a palace there

2

A significant feature of Crete in the Bronze Age was the growth of towns and their palaces. Here we see a wing of the palace at Mallia, with its central court and the altar in the foreground.

in ancient times. But," he added, "those of us who live here know better."

The man "poking around" the little hamlet that lay three miles inland was Arthur Evans. He certainly seemed to be doing an odd thing, for Knossos appeared to be no different from any other place on the island — just wheat fields and olive trees and a little cluster of houses. And yet, when Evans died during World War II, he died as Sir Arthur Evans, perhaps the world's most famous archeologist. He had excavated at Knossos a royal palace that covered six acres, and a paved sidewalk that led to smaller palaces and to villas once occupied by powerful officials. Although we know how much land the royal palace covered, we do not know how high the building was because, while it is possible to walk up the quadruple staircase today, the structure ends in midair.

Evans' achievement seems almost incredible, and it becomes even more so when we consider that he found altogether a complete

The Palace of Minos covers six acres and is a maze of corridors, halls, and rooms. The steep, narrow staircase in the rear was for slaves.

epoch, or period, of civilization that had lasted for two thousand years. The palace that Evans found represents the height of the Bronze Age civilization in Crete itself. Not only is the building architecturally fascinating, but when Evans uncovered it he found it full of magnificent treasures that revealed exquisite taste. There were wonderful examples of metalwork and pottery, carvings in ivory, and most important of all, perhaps, colorful frescoes, or wall paintings, that showed how people lived and dressed and worshiped during the Bronze Age. Thanks to Evans, this period of legend and romance has come alive; it is no longer a myth but a historical fact, and despite its tremendous age, it is recognized as one of the most civilized moments in man's long history.

Since all true knowledge of the Bronze Age had vanished from men's minds for so many years, how did Evans ever happen to discover the things he did? What in the world did he have to go by? Actually, he had a good deal, for he was a highly educated man.

In the first place, Evans had history to guide him. He had read many legends of Knossos and Crete, and knew that though a legend is not straight history, it often contains a kernel of historical fact. For example, there is the legend of a powerful Cretan king at Knossos. The king's name was Minos, and he had an amazing bull, half animal, half human, called the Minotaur, which means Minos' bull. The king kept the animal in an underground stable known as the labyrinth — a building of intricate, winding passageways in which it is very easy to get lost.

The story says that the Greek city of Athens had to send seven boys and seven girls every year to Knossos, where they were thrown into the labyrinth and devoured by the bull. Finally the Athenian hero, Theseus, said that this had gone on long enough. He offered to go to Crete with the next shipload of young people.

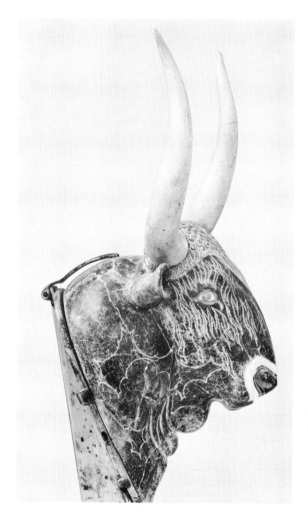

A black steatite rhyton in the form of a bull's head, from Knossos. The nostrils are of shell, the eyes of rock crystal, and the horns of gilded wood. The hair between the horns is in relief; the mottled hide is suggested by incised lines.
HIRMER FOTOARCHIV

When he landed, Theseus met the king's daughter, Ariadne, and they fell in love with each other at sight. That night Theseus slipped into the labyrinth carrying a dagger and a ball of string, both given him by Ariadne. As he made his way along the winding passageways, he unrolled the string so that he could follow it back to where he had entered the labyrinth. When he met the Minotaur, he killed it with Ariadne's dagger. Theseus and Ariadne then fled from Crete in a boat.

6

There is the legend. The historical fact is that Athens was once under Crete's influence, but finally threw the influence off. And so Evans figured that there must be something — certainly something more than a stable — to be discovered at Knossos.

Evans had other things to guide him, too, all of them familiar to archeologists. As he wandered around Knossos he picked up engraved seals and broken pieces of pottery. These and their decorations resembled the seals and bits of pottery found by another archeologist, Schliemann, at Troy and elsewhere. These objects told Evans, even before he started to dig, that Knossos and the whole island of Crete had once belonged to a civilization that had been widespread and from which had come many legends. The story of Theseus and the Minotaur was one of these, as we already know. Another was the story of the Trojan War.

The Trojan War

IT WAS the blind Greek poet Homer who told the story of the Trojan War many centuries ago. The war, so went the tale, started with a banquet given by some goddesses. The Goddess of Discord, who had not been invited, tossed among the guests an apple labeled, "To the Fairest." Each goddess claimed the apple, and since none could agree as to whom it rightfully belonged, they decided to ask Paris, son of Priam, the king of Troy, to be the judge.

Paris awarded the apple to Aphrodite, known to the Romans as Venus, because she promised him the most beautiful woman in the world. Naturally, Aphrodite and her friends were pleased with Paris' choice, but the other goddesses hated the young man. And so the gods, who lived forever on Mount Olympus in northern Greece, were

7

divided into two camps, some favoring Paris' city of Troy, some against it.

The most beautiful woman in the world was said to be Helen, wife of Menelaus, king of Sparta. When Paris went traveling a few years after awarding Aphrodite the apple, he stayed at the king's palace. He and Helen fell in love and ran off to Troy together. According to the legend, the Greeks then went to war against Troy in order to bring Helen back to Greece. Today we can get beneath the legend and see that the Greeks of the mainland were really after something more important than the rescue of Helen when they sailed to attack Troy.

Troy was located in the northwestern corner of Asia Minor (now Turkey) near the entrance to the Hellespont, or the Dardanelles, as we call the narrow strait today. It was more of a robber fortress than a city, and its location made it easy for the Trojans to prey on land traffic between Europe and Asia, as well as on ships plying between the Aegean and Black Seas. The Greeks were eager to put a stop to this.

The legend says that Menelaus sent word to his brother, Agamemnon, that Paris had run away with Helen. Agamemnon was the powerful king of Mycenae, and the recognized leader of his time. Enraged by Paris' daring, he swore vengeance against Troy. Finally, a Greek armada sailed across the Aegean, landed at Troy, and, after ten years of fighting, took the city with the help of some of the gods. Homer wrote one epic poem (a long poem on a lofty theme) about a part of the fighting. This was the *Iliad*; another poem, the *Odyssey*, told how one of the Greek heroes, Odysseus (whom the Romans called Ulysses), spent ten more years wandering back to his island of Ithaca.

The cemetery at Knossos has yielded this bronze sword, about two feet in length. On its gold handle lions pursuing goats are etched. The knob, or pommel, is of translucent agate (a chalcedony).

HIRMER FOTOARCHIV

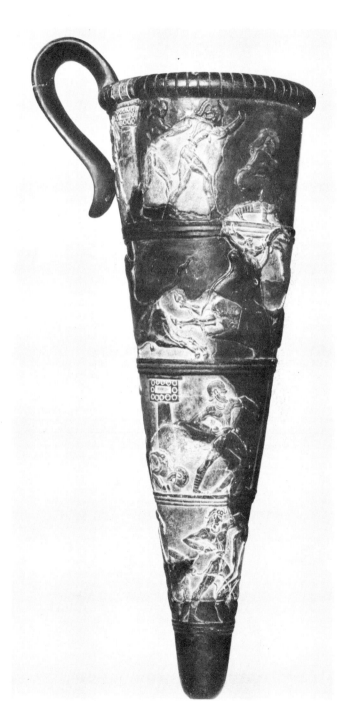

A rhyton, or drinking cup, of black steatite from Hagia Triada, illustrating the Minoan love of sports. The top panel shows wrestlers; the second, bull-jumping; the bottom two panels show boxers, some of whom wear helmets.

Another Myth Is Tested

FOR MANY centuries everyone thought of the Trojan War as a myth, beautiful and heroic, of course, but something out of Homer's own mind. In the last century, however, a merchant prince of Germany, Heinrich Schliemann by name, decided to test the myth. Schliemann's father had been a minister, the boy had grown up on Homer, and now that he had made a fortune, he decided to spend his money investigating the sites of Homer's tales.

Schliemann is known to history as the father of scientific excavation. Many people before him had robbed graves, but it was Schliemann who first dug carefully and recorded carefully so that the history of a place would be reconstructed. He found vast treasures at Troy; in fact, he found nine cities piled one on top of the other, the Troy of the famous War among them.

When archeologists are hunting for a lost city, they look for two things — parts of buildings still standing, and mounds of earth. A mound of earth may seem an odd clue to the location of a city, but archeologists know that the treasures they are seeking often lie buried under such mounds. The nine cities of which Troy was one made a pretty big mound, and it provides a perfect illustration of the way a mound comes into existence.

The Trojans, like most people in antiquity, built their houses of mud bricks that had been baked in the sun. Such bricks, unlike those baked in an oven, disintegrate rather easily. If there is no roof over them to protect them from the rain, they disintegrate very promptly. Fortunately for us, the Trojans did not place their bricks directly on the ground where puddles of rain would dissolve them. Instead, they placed them on fieldstones, and these stones remain to tell us the

11

shapes of the houses and the size and number of rooms inside them.

Like other people of early days, the Trojans had almost no idea of sanitation. Meat and oysters made up a large part of their diet, and when they ate these, they tossed the bones and shells on the earthen floor of the house and left them there. Periodically they got rid of the rubbish by covering it up with another layer of earth — a sort of spring-cleaning.

If a cow died in one of the narrow alleys that served as streets in Troy, nobody did anything about it. The carcass was simply left there, along with other rubbish. As the debris collected, the level of the street slowly rose. In time it rose so high that it was difficult for a man to walk out of his house onto the street. Finally there was nothing he could do but knock down his house and build another. But instead of carting away the remains of his old house, he simply leveled them off and built another house on top of them. Slowly he was creating a mound.

Something quite different happened when a city was destroyed by fire or sacked by the enemy. Then the entire city would be rebuilt, and in the debris beneath it would be buried pottery and other forgotten possessions of the previous inhabitants.

Through the centuries, the Trojans built no less than nine cities in this way, forming little by little the great mound under which Schliemann found the city nobody believed had ever existed.

After Schliemann had unearthed Troy, he went to Mycenae, another city of legend. There he found treasures similar to those he had found in Troy, but richer beyond comparison. Their similarity, however, told him that the two cities had belonged to the same civilization. And when Evans later picked up those seals and pottery fragments at Knossos, he knew that his site of legend had also been part of that bigger civilization.

The Palace of King Minos

IN CRETE, civilized life started about 3000 B.C., the beginning of the Bronze Age. Although we now have an immense amount of information about the early Cretans, we do not know yet who they were or where they came from. Probably they did not belong to the Indo-European branch of the human race, as did the ancient Greeks and Italians. We do not know whether a king named Minos really lived, but we can make ourselves understood more easily if we have labels for the things we discuss. Sir Arthur Evans was very sensible when he took the name of the legendary king, Minos, and applied it to the monarch who supposedly lived in the palace at Knossos in the days of its greatest splendor, 1600 B.C.

Evans even made an adjective of the king's name — "Minoan." He used this adjective to describe the whole Bronze Age civilization of Crete and the civilization of all other places under its influence, whether it was mainland Greece, the islands of the Aegean, the coast of Asia Minor, or any other place throughout the Mediterranean. During this amazing period of history, Minoan cultural influences and trade spread far and wide from Crete.

About 1800 B.C. — some two centuries before Minoan civilization reached its height — the king reigning at Knossos saw his chance to turn the whole town into his own palace. He moved the population off to a distance, turned the old town square into the court of the palace, and brought together the buildings that had stood around the square to form the palace itself. Changes and additions were made in time, so that when Knossos reached its very height in 1600 B.C., a truly remarkable structure had been created.

13

TO CANDIA
VILLA ARIADNE 100 METERS

TO PORT

VILLAGE OF MAKRYTEICHOS

THE LITTLE PALACE

M.M.I. DEPOSITS

UNEXPLORED MANSION

THE ROYAL VILLA

METOCHI

MINOAN ROAD

MAGAZINES OF ARMOURY AND HOUSES

NORTH HOUSE

INN

THEATRAL AREA

NORTH PILLAR HALL

HOUSE OF THE FRESCOES

NORTH EAST HOUSE

GUARDIAN'S HOUSE

WEST

EARLY HOUSES

WALLED PIT

COURT

THE CENTRAL COURT PALACE

OLD COURSE OF MINOAN ROAD

5 Kilometers to Candia

THRESHING FLOOR

EAST HOUSE

HOUSE OF THE CHANCEL

M.M. HOUSES

SOUTH EAST HOUSE

OLD ROAD TO CANDIA

BRIDGE END

STEPPED PORTICO

MINOAN HOUSES

OLD COURSE OF STREAM

VLYCHIA

STREAM

PRESUMED MINOAN ROAD FROM SOUTH

PIERS OF MINOAN VIADUCT

NEW MAIN ROAD

CARAVAN-SERAI

HOUSE OF TURKISH BEY ORIGINAL HEADQUARTERS

Well (M.M.III L.M.I)

VLYCHIA SPRING

SPILIOPOTAMOS OR KASSABANOS (ANCIENT KAIRATOS)

HILL OF GYPSADES

PALACE OF MINOS AND SURROUNDINGS

MINOAN HOUSES

SCALE OF METRES

100   50   0   100

MINOAN HOUSES

GARDEN

AND

ORCHARD

MINOAN GYPSUM QUARRY WITH SUBTERRANEAN EXTENSION

M.M.I. DEPOSITS

MINOAN HOUSES

FROM ARKHANES

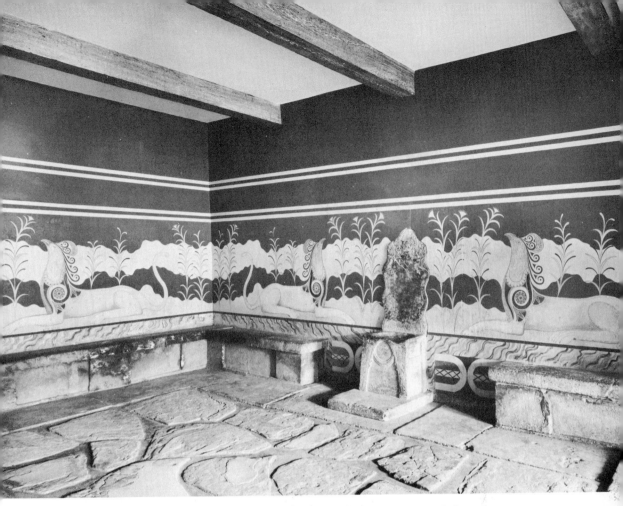

The throne room of the Palace of Minos, where the Priest King met with his advisers. The plaster on the walls is painted a deep red, with representations of flowers and griffins.

The palace of Minos was built of handsome blocks of gypsum (a mineral notable for its crystals) which supported rough upper walls covered with plaster. The central court, which was once the old public square, is two hundred feet long, eighty-five feet wide, and open to the sky. Facing the court are the rooms of state, the most striking of which is the throne room. This room gives a general impression of

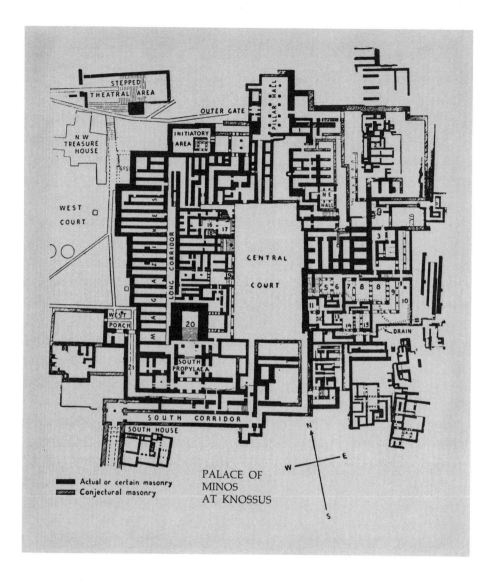

PALACE OF
MINOS
AT KNOSSUS

■ Actual or certain masonry
▨ Conjectural masonry

1. Guard room
2. Royal pottery room
3. School room
4. Lower east-west corridor
5. Light area
6. Hall of the Colonnades
7. Light Area
8. Hall of the Double Axes
9. Portico
10. Light area
11. Court of the Distaffs

12. w.c.
13. Bath
14. Queen's Megaron
15. Light area
16. Room of the Throne
17. Ante-room
18. Lustral basin
19. Shrine
20. Grand Staircase up to Piano Nobile
21. Corridor of the Procession

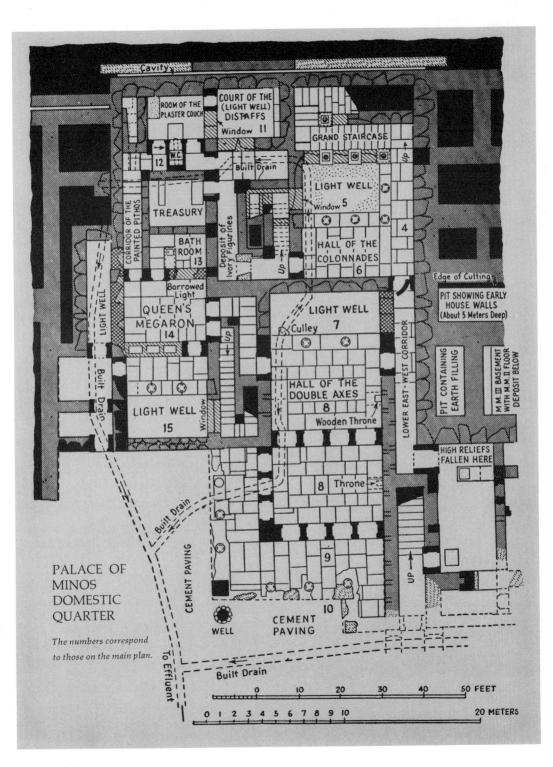

Cavity

ROOM OF THE
PLASTER COUCH

COURT OF THE
(LIGHT WELL) DISTAFFS
Window 11

GRAND STAIRCASE

W.C.

12

Built Drain

LIGHT WELL
Window 5

CORRIDOR OF THE PAINTED PITHOS

TREASURY

Deposit of Ivory Figurines

4

BATH
ROOM
13

HALL OF THE
COLONNADES
6

Edge of Cutting

PIT SHOWING EARLY
HOUSE WALLS
(About 5 Meters Deep)

LIGHT WELL

Borrowed
Light

QUEEN'S
MEGARON
14

LIGHT WELL
Culley   7

Up

LOWER EAST-WEST CORRIDOR

PIT CONTAINING
EARTH FILLING

M.M. III BASEMENT WITH M.M. II FLOOR DEPOSIT BELOW

Built Drain

Up

HALL OF THE
DOUBLE AXES
8

LIGHT WELL
15   Window

Wooden Throne

HIGH RELIEFS
FALLEN HERE

Built Drain

8   Throne

PALACE OF
MINOS
DOMESTIC
QUARTER

The numbers correspond
to those on the main plan.

Built Drain

9

UP

CEMENT PAVING

To Effluent

WELL

10

CEMENT
PAVING

Built Drain

0   10   20   30   40   50 FEET

0 1 2 3 4 5 6 7 8 9 10   20 METERS

On a wall of the Palace of Minos, the artist first modeled (in stucco relief) and then painted (in vivid reds and blues) the Priest King of Knossos. He stands against a background of lilies and wears jewelry, a loin cloth, and a crown of flowers and feathers.

PHILIP GENDREAU

subdued and simple splendor. The splendor is due to the frescoes, or wall paintings, which show plants and mythical creatures, called griffins, against a deep red background. The simple stone throne, a mere seat with a high back, stands in sharp contrast to the immense influence of the Minoan civilization. Flanking the throne are stone benches, covered with red and white plaster, where the king's advisers sat. This leads us to believe that the king's power was limited by the nobles.

Connected with the throne room is a watertight tank. People in ancient days were eager to wash away their sins, and since this ceremony was performed in Crete in the presence of the king, we must think of him as a combination of priest and king. Probably he was the representative of the Great Mother goddess, the chief deity of that time.

At different seasons of the year, Crete has intense heat and very cold winds, which helps to explain why the outside rooms of the palace seldom have windows. Light and air came from light wells inside the house. These resembled elevator shafts with the tops removed. When it rained, the Cretans stretched skins above the openings. If they did not do this before the rains began, there were elaborate drainage systems to carry away the water.

The sprawling palace of King Minos had many comfortable rooms, but none more luxurious than the private dwelling rooms of the royal family. Evans called this part of the palace the Domestic Quarter. In the larger of the two main rooms of the quarter he found a great, bronze double ax. Several sketches of the ax are scratched on the walls of the room, which leads us to believe that the weapon was a symbol of the king's power. This room, known as the Hall of the Double Axes, was probably where the king relaxed with his family and intimate friends.

A corner of the Hall of the Double Axes, with its throne and representations of huge figure-eight shields.

Both the Hall of the Double Axes and the Queen's Megaron, or Hall of State, which was connected with it by a short corridor, have their own light wells. The walls of the two rooms are covered with fine paintings, often in vivid colors, of dolphins, fish, marine designs, such as floating seaweed, as well as formal designs of rosettes and spirals, and depictions of human figures.

In a room next to the Queen's Megaron was found a painted terra-cotta bathtub. It has no plumbing connections, but in those days there were slaves to pour the water in and bail it out again. Further down the corridor was a water closet. It should not surprise us to find the convenience of flush toilets in that ancient city, for the Minoans had such engineering skill that they were able to build a reservoir and conduct water to the palace by means of an aqueduct several miles long.

An appealing feature of the Queen's Megaron is a private staircase that enabled the queen to go upstairs without disturbing the men in the Hall of the Double Axes. As a rule, however, men and women together took the main east-west corridor to the Hall of the Colon-

The main east-west corridor, leading from the Hall of the Double Axes, ends here in the Hall of the Colonnades and the grand quadruple staircase. A window opens on the light wall.

HIRMER FOTOARCHIV

nades; from this point the grand quadruple staircase wound upward. Controlled magnificence in good taste is the overwhelming impression we receive as we walk along the majestic corridors, courts, and rooms of the palace.

The Minoans' love of nature is clearly shown in their exquisitely cut gems and sealstones, in the vividly colorful frescoes and pottery, so full of imagination and action. Occasionally, as we look at the frescoes, we feel that some "modern" art is not quite so modern, for the Minoan artist did not hesitate to make plants grow upside down or to change red roses to green, if he thought this would help the effect. In other words, an exact reproduction of nature is never necessary (besides, a photograph will do it better) — rather, the artist must improve on nature.

One of the most beautiful Minoan frescoes shows a lifelike cat creeping through the rushes toward an unsuspecting pheasant. Another merely represents a simple blue bird resting amid rocks and roses. In still other frescoes we see crocuses, flying fish, men and women with refined features.

The pottery exhibits the same love of color and nature. A striking vase, for example, has two dark brown octopuses floating across its light surface. Most of the movable objects have been placed in the Herakleion Museum, which, as a result, is the greatest museum of its kind on earth.

Archeology can tell us many things, but there are some things it cannot tell us. It can tell us that Knossos had a king, that he had advisers, that the artists had imagination and loved color and nature, which must also have been true of the people who looked at their works. But archeology cannot give us their conversations and literature. For these things we need writing that we can understand.

A dark brown octopus, amid seaweed and cuttlefish, floats across the light surface of a vase; an illustration of the Minoan love of nature and of the artist's ability to relate pattern to the shape of the vase. From the American excavations at Gournia in eastern Crete.

CANDIA MUSEUM,
ATHENS, GREECE

The Harvester's Vase from the palace at Hagia Triada (the lower half is missing). It is of black steatite, a soft mineral. The artist who carved it has been able to suggest exuberant life and motion. An elderly man in ceremonial dress leads a happy throng after the harvest has been gathered.

HIRMER FOTOARCHIV

The Minoans did indeed write on clay tablets. Theirs was a strange script, called syllabic, with characters representing syllables rather than single characters. For convenience, scholars have named it Linear A. Its secret has not yet been cracked, but as more and more young students are attracted to the field of archeology, someone is bound to discover the key to Linear A.

23

In this wall painting from the Palace of Minos, we see that one member of an acrobatic team has landed behind the bull and is about to catch another, who is doing a flip on the bull's back; he in turn will try to catch the third member, who just now has seized the bull by the horns.

Minoan Life

THE MINOANS, it seems abundantly clear, were a gay and carefree people. In the evening, when the rooms were illuminated by oil lamps of porphyry and other colored stones, they played games that resembled parcheesi. An exceptionally grand gaming board has been found, made of crystal, ivory, blue paste, gold, and silver.

During the day, the Minoans boxed and wrestled, and teams of young men and women competed periodically in bull jumping. This was not bullfighting; no animals were hurt, though perhaps at the end of the festivities they were sacrificed to the gods, providing the spectators with a good meal, to boot. We must think of a young acrobat as seizing a charging bull by the horns; as the angry animal tossed his head upward, the acrobat would do a somersault over the bull's back and land on the ground behind it.

The ordinary dress of the men consisted of a simple loincloth with an apron. The women, however, wore corsets, skirts that were bell-shaped or flounced, and bodices that were open in front, with high collars at the back. They also used cosmetics. Both sexes wore sandals, rings, and seals that hung from the neck or wrist. So elegant was the dress of the women, so elaborate their hairdo, as paintings portray them watching religious and athletic events, that observers have often likened them to the court ladies at Versailles in the days of Louis XIV.

Swings, pullcarts, and other toys survive to suggest the life of very young children. As the children grew up, the more privileged ones attended school in the palace. The schoolroom is still there, with small stone seats for the pupils, a large one in front for the teacher.

A lively bull-jumper from Knossos. Though the ivory is worn in places, we can see the detailed attention given to fingers, veins, and muscles.

HIRMER FOTOARCHIV

Clothing and many other things that we would buy in a store were often made at home in ancient days. This is a wine-press in the house of a Minoan noble. The grapes were crushed in the clay bowl, while the juice ran out into the large jar below it. A stone drain can be seen in the paved floor to the rear.

The palace was, in fact, practically a self-contained village. It had its own olive press, arsenal, workshops, and storerooms. More than twenty magazines — long, narrow storage rooms — have been found, full of immense vases. Originally, these contained wheat, wine, and olive oil, which the Minoans used to pay their taxes, for they had no coined money. The king exchanged this produce for goods from Egypt and Syria.

The Palace of Minos at Knossos has more than twenty of these long magazines or storage rooms. The large vases originally held wheat and olive oil — taxes paid in kind — which the king then exchanged for goods from Egypt and Syria. The plaster on the walls shows the marks of a fire.

The famous Minoan Great Mother goddess — also called a Snake-Goddess. Six and a half inches high, she is carved in ivory, with gold decoration on her dress and originally on her crown. The snakes, also of gold, were regarded as protectors of the household, hence as good luck.

Although the king himself acted as high priest of the Minoan religion, women played an important part in the actual worship. Paintings show them conducting formal dances in sacred groves and in the theater of the palace. We also have numerous sculptures of the Great Mother goddess, who is sometimes called a Snake-Goddess, because snakes, symbols of good luck, are often in her hands. The most extraordinary of these Snake-Goddess sculptures is in the Museum of Fine Arts in Boston. It is only about six and a half inches high, exquisitely carved in ivory, and shows a goddess of austerity and breeding with gold snakes in her hands and gold ornaments on her dress. Ceremonies in her honor were conducted in small shrines, for great religious temples were unknown to Minoan Crete.

The Minoan Peace

THE PALACE of Minos could not have been built without a strong, centralized government; nor could it have stood through the generations without the blessings of peace. By far the most amazing thing about the palace is the complete absence of fortification walls; one tower is practically the only sign of defense structures. This proves, in the first place, that the Cretans had no foreign foes and that their navy controlled at least the nearby seas, a fact various legends also emphasize.

The second thing proven by the lack of fortifications is that the people of Knossos had no domestic enemies to fear. It is not likely that their king ruled the entire island directly, but he doubtless controlled it through princes who were directly responsible to him. When we think of all the wars that would bring destruction to Europe in the future, it is downright thrilling to visit various small towns in Crete and see the concrete results of the famous Minoan Peace. For instance, at Gournia, you can run up and down the streets, turn here and there into the houses, go up the stone steps to the second floor, or down into the cellar, stroll around the palace, without seeing a single scar of battle. Just think of it! For two centuries or more this town and its neighbors did not know the horrors of war.

The population of Knossos, together with its nearby harbor town, has been estimated at fifty thousand — 25 per cent larger than present-day Herakleion. Although it was the largest city of Minoan Crete, it was by no means the only large one, as the Italian excavators of Phaistos, on the south side of the island, have shown. In Phaistos stands a palace that rivals Knossos in almost every respect. The magnificence of the site once so stirred a French prime minister that he exclaimed that Phaistos is as close to heaven as anyone can ever get on earth.

A paved road, with bridges at appropriate points, connected Phaistos and Knossos. Travelers who could afford it were carried on a litter, or went by horse and chariot or four-wheeled carts. At the Knossos end of the road were an inn and a footbath for weary travelers.

Knossos' leadership of the Bronze Age ended in 1500 B.C., when the city was captured by Greeks from Mycenae. It may seem strange that this island city did not have a navy strong enough to hold off the Mycenaean invasion. The astounding truth is that the Minoan navy had probably been badly damaged by a tidal wave, the result of an earthquake at the island of Thera, which is known to have occurred at that time.

Thera is unique among the many beautiful islands of the Aegean Sea. Originally, it was a volcano rising right up out of the water, but the eruption in 1500 B.C. blew away the cone. Today ships anchor in what was once the cone of the volcano. At one side of the cone there is a tiny island, still smoking. The rest of Thera consists of the original rim of the volcano, broken here and there so that you can sail between the fragments. The sides of the rim are high, precipitous, blackened rocks, reminding one of imaginary pictures of Hades.

The explosion of Thera probably set off a tidal wave that damaged the Minoan navy. The Mycenaeans no doubt chose the Minoans' moment of weakness for their attack on Knossos. They were able to hold on to the island only until about 1400 B.C., but in the meantime they had established themselves as the new leaders of the Bronze Age world, a position they held until the end of the age itself.

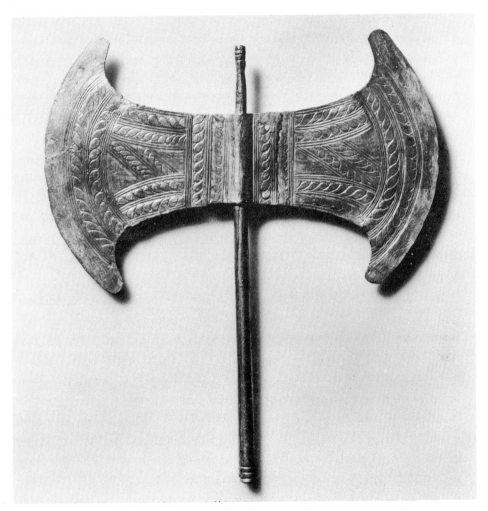

Minoan religious ceremonies were conducted in sacred groves, mountain caves, and small shrines in private houses; there were no large temples. This impressive gold double ax was used originally for the slaying of a sacrificial animal, but came to symbolize the Great Mother goddess and also the king's power.

Unearthing A Lost City

IT IS EASIER to understand Mycenae and the entire Bronze Age if we know how archeologists go about recovering the past. There is nothing mysterious about it, though some of the problems do seem impossible to solve. Certainly the work is full of romance and excitement.

The chief difference between excavating in Greece and certain other lands — Mesopotamia (modern Iraq), for example — is that an expedition in Greece does not have to be organized from abroad and then, at great cost, be brought into the country. For many years various countries, including Britain, France, Germany, Italy, and Sweden, have maintained archeological schools right in Athens. The American School of Classical Studies, founded in 1881, has conducted several distinguished excavations. These have been in the Agora, or civic center of ancient Athens, at Corinth (where Brown University is cooperating), and at sites next to Mycenae in the Argive Plain (Argolis).

Because of these foreign schools, and the great Greek Archeological Society itself, trained top personnel are always at hand. Another fortunate fact is that excavating has been going on for so long in Greece that there are plenty of skilled workmen available. It is not easy to break in an inexperienced workman and explain to him how he must avoid scratching a statue, for example.

After the site to be excavated has been decided upon, the staff who will be in charge of the excavation assembles. At the top is the director, with perhaps half a dozen assistants. If it is an American expedition, the assistants are likely to be American graduate students.

Excavation involves destruction; things can never be put back in place. For this reason, everything that is dug up must be carefully recorded. The records must include not only the exact spot where the object was found, but also the depth at which it was buried and its original relationship to other objects. Only in this way can the history of the site be reconstructed. The archeologist is neither a grave robber nor a gold seeker; like all scholars and scientists, he is a seeker after truth.

An architect is an important member of any archeological expedition; diggers are bound to come upon buildings of one kind or another, and these must be sketched for the records. There must be a photographer to take pictures of all kinds of objects. Then, too, there will be work for various technicians, especially pot-menders. Pottery in vast amounts is the one thing archeologists are bound to find. Much of the pottery will be broken, but a smart boy can clean the fragments and fit them together, often making a complete vase.

The number of workmen will be determined by the site that is to be excavated. The American School hired several hundred workmen in the Athenian Agora, but thirty would be average for a Bronze Age site. There will have to be a foreman in charge of the workmen, and this will probably be a Greek of long experience.

The first thing the workmen do is to dig a long trench. Some of the men break the earth with picks, others shovel it into baskets. Still others carry the baskets off to the dump.

As the workmen find fragments of pottery in the earth they are digging, they toss the fragments into the nearest of a number of baskets lined up alongside the trench. Each of these baskets has a label that bears the number of the trench, the basket's location beside the trench, and the trench's depth at that point. There is a good chance that the fragments of a vase have not strayed very far from one another, and that the pot-mender will be able to find them and fit them together. In any case, the pottery will be carefully studied for whatever secrets it may yield about dates.

How can pottery tell us anything about dates? There is nothing very complicated about it, really. Men who lived in ancient times

A rock-crystal dish from Mycenae, with a graceful swan's neck and head as handle.

used pottery far more than we do — for cups, pitchers, dishes, and many other things. Wherever they lived, they left behind masses of it. Ancient pottery is practically indestructible, for it was baked in ovens. It will break, yes, but the fragments will remain intact. Archeologists call them potsherds, or sherds, for short. Each generation had its own way of shaping and decorating its pottery, and by studying it, we can learn a great deal about the makers' sense of line and color. More important, however, is the fact that with long study archeologists have been able to date the pottery by its decoration. It follows, therefore, that pottery of the same type will date everything that is found with it. Scholars call this relative chronology, or dating. In the case of Crete, the actual dates in terms of years B.C. are possible, for Crete imported some objects from Egypt, and all these are precisely dated because of the wonderfully accurate Egyptian calendar that runs back to 3000 B.C.

The duty of the archeologist is to supervise and record the daily work, to make sure that everything the workmen have found is safely stored and, eventually, using the notes he has made on the site, to publish his findings in a learned journal. An excavation may continue for years, and from time to time a scholar will publish a book covering perhaps just one aspect of the findings, such as the sculpture. It is in this way that scholars throughout the civilized world can keep abreast of the advance of knowledge of ancient times and pass it on to their students.

A vase of alabaster (a translucent gypsum), with three looped handles.

HIRMER FOTOARCHIV

Most of the gold and bronze treasures found at Mycenae came from this "Grave Circle" — the royal cemetery on the side of the citadel. The entrance to the Treasury of Atreus appears as a gash on the hillside beyond; in the distance, the Argive Plain and the mountains of Arcadia.

A Problem—and How It Is Solved

SUPPOSE we take one of the problems an archeologist has to solve, and see how he solves it. Among the important things he looks for is a cemetery. The tombs where the ancients buried their dead tell us about their burial customs, what people believed about the next world, and something about their architecture. Most people of ancient times, including the Mycenaeans, believed that men needed in the next world the same kind of things they had used in this world, things such as cups, knives, jewelry, mirrors, and so on. These artifacts, as they are called, tell us not only how people were buried, but also a great deal about how they lived and their ability as artists and craftsmen.

The Mycenaeans used various types of graves, but among the most interesting were the tombs of the nobles. Several hundred of these have been excavated in and around Mycenae, and about as many more remain to be dug. The question is, of course, how does an archeologist discover an ancient grave? He cannot tear up the countryside with a steam shovel or a bulldozer, for that would ruin everything. His duty, as an excavator, is to leave things in exactly the same condition as they were originally.

The nobles of Mycenae were buried in what are called rock-cut chamber tombs. When a noble wanted to build a tomb for his family, he took his slaves out to a hillside, where there were probably other tombs, and told them to dig a trench into the heart of the hill. A trench might be more than a hundred feet long, known to archeologists as a *dromos*. The earthen sides of the *dromos* had a "batter" — that is, they slanted outward from the top, so that the distance across the top was less than at the bottom.

37

The Treasury of Atreus, the most splendid monument of Mycenaean Greece. Well-cut blocks laid in regular courses (known as ashlar construction) line the sides of the entrance passage, or dromos, which is 115 feet long and 20 feet wide. 1300 B.C.

Within the chamber of the tomb at Dendra, the excavators dug away the relatively soft, disturbed earth, revealing the grave and skeleton of the rich and powerful king.

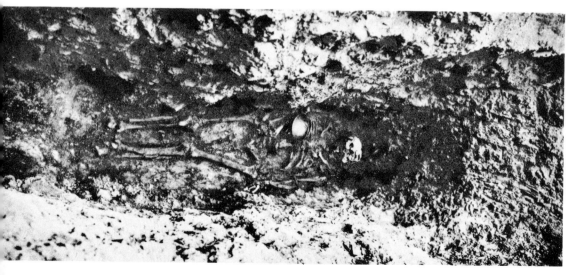

The earthen floor of the *dromos* sloped gradually downward until, at a certain point, the builders decided to dig a doorway. Beyond the doorway they dug a chamber, thirty or forty feet in diameter, out of the native rock. Such a chamber is really an artificial cave cut out of the soft rock of a hillside. Twenty people might be buried in it.

At Dendra, near Mycenae, Swedish excavators found a tomb of exceptional wealth. In one pit in the floor the king and queen had been buried; another pit held the bones of a young daughter; human bones, a dog's skull and other animal bones filled the third pit; and the fourth was used for sacrifices in honor of the dead. An exquisitely beautiful gold cup with octopuses in relief was found beside the king; also a gold-lined silver cup with bulls in relief, gems, rings, spearheads, knives, and bronze swords with gold hilts and pommels of ivory or agate (a variegated translucent mineral). There was also an ostrich egg, imported from Egypt, that has a silver neck and decorations of gold, bronze, and glass paste.

Beside the queen had been placed a gold-lined silver cup decorated with bulls' heads inlaid in gold and niello (a dark metallic alloy of sulfur with silver or copper); a carnelian gem, a gold box, and sixty-one gold beads of a necklace.

A nearby grave contained, among other things, lamps of steatite (a soft mineral of a grayish green color), boars' tusks (which made a terrifying decoration on leather helmets), beads of glass paste, twenty-four bronze vessels, four bronze mirrors, knives, arrowheads, and a six-pronged fishing spear. It is easy to understand why all the earth from such an excavation must be carefully sifted.

When finally a tomb was full and the family decided to close it, workmen gathered fieldstones and placed them in the doorway.

Embossed dolphins, octopuses cover the surface of the gold cup that had settled down on the ribs of the Dendra king.

Then they filled the *dromos* with earth. Soon the grass began to grow over the tomb, and nobody — certainly neither you nor I — can tell that a tomb had once stood here or there in the hillside. Nothing but earth confronts the visitor. It is easy to find out, however, if there is a tomb under the grass if you know how to go about it.

It is a very fortunate fact for archeologists that earth, when once disturbed, even if it was disturbed thousands of years ago, is softer to the feel of a pick than undisturbed earth, or hardpan. Archeologists call this undisturbed earth *stereo*. If he thinks that a particular hill beside the Argive Plain contains tombs, the archeologist takes some workmen and digs a trench around it. The top of the earth may at some time have been disturbed by a plow, so he first digs two or three feet down in order to get below it. He may be in for a disappointment, for the subsoil may be good and hard. This means that he has *stereo*, earth that has never been touched by man, and he will find nothing. Either he has chosen the wrong hill, or he has dug the trench too far up the hillside. So he starts again, but farther down the hillside.

Once again the picks go in hard, but then suddenly — and it is a

40

breathtaking moment — the earth is relatively soft. Considering what part of the world he is in, he has most certainly discovered the *dromos* of an ancient tomb.

Now the archeologist tells his workmen to start digging a trench into the hill — that is, to commence clearing out the *dromos*. As the trench widens, he will occasionally call a halt to the work and drive the hunting knife that every excavator carries into the bank of earth at either side. If the earth is still soft, he keeps digging; but if it is hard, he stops, for it would be a dreadful thing to spend all that effort digging away earth that no man has ever touched.

Little by little, the entire *dromos* is cleared. There is the batter of the earthen walls, the sloping earthen floor. There, at last, is the doorway to the tomb, filled with fieldstones. When he has photo-

The dromos of the tomb, its doorway blocked with field stones.

HIRMER FOTOARCHIV

graphed, drawn, and studied the doorway, the archeologist takes the fieldstones out.

It would be foolish to suppose that the archeologist is not human and full of excited curiosity to see the interior of the tomb. Fallen rock debris, however, will be the thing most likely to greet him. But at last the debris is removed, he digs out the burial pits, finds the skeletons (generally very well preserved), and all the objects buried with them. A good job has been done.

Archeology — which is one branch of ancient history — needs more and more students. The best way to prepare yourself in school is to study Latin (and Greek, if you can get it), because you are immediately and wonderfully introduced to ancient life and thought.

A gold diadem buried with a Mycenaean princess. It is decorated with circles filled with rosettes or bosses (protruberant ornaments).

A gold death mask of a
Mycenaean prince. It was
found in the Grave Circle
of the citadel.

Dog's heads serve as handles on the gracefully shaped gold cup from Mycenae, shown on opposite page.
HIRMER FOTOARCHIV

Mycenae, "Rich in Gold"

IT WAS Homer who called Mycenae rich in gold, but even in his wildest imagination the blind poet fell far short of the reality. The exact reasons for Mycenae's wealth and power are not entirely clear. We know that there were copper mines in the hills around the city, but even more important, probably, was Mycenae's location. Like Knossos, Troy, and other places, it was near the sea for purposes of trade, but it was not right on the coast where pirates could suddenly appear and plunder it.

Moreover, Mycenae dominated the pass between the Argive Plain and the Gulf of Corinth, one of the main trade routes of southern Greece (the Peloponnesus). Boats would land their goods at Nauplia, and then donkeys would transport the various articles to Corinth. At that point they would be transshipped across the Gulf and sent on their way to Delphi, Thebes, and other spots in Central Greece. The control of this traffic greatly enriched Mycenae.

Although Schliemann was the first to excavate at Mycenae, archeologists have continued the work to the present day, and much still remains to be done. Most of the movable objects have been placed in the National Museum of Athens, where they fill an enormous room and leave visitors breathless with their glistening splendor.

A rhyton (drinking cup) of silver and gold, from the Grave Circle of Mycenae's citadel.

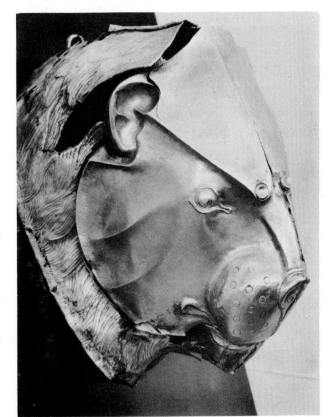

A magnificent rhyton from Mycenae, about 1500 B.C. It was hammered out of a single sheet of gold. The lion's head is portrayed both naturally and decoratively.

The Mycenaeans were Greeks whose forebears started coming into what we now call Greece about 2000 B.C. They mingled with the earlier inhabitants (whose identity is unknown to us), quickly absorbed the cultural influences spreading from Minoan Crete, and developed their own inborn gifts.

By 1600 B.C., when Knossos dominated a wide world, Mycenae was the chief city of the Greek mainland, civilized and rich. On the side of their main hill, or citadel, the kings created a cemetery whose contents form perhaps the greatest gold treasure from any Bronze Age site in the world.

Schliemann found the royal graves surrounded by an impressive circular wall. In the tombs there were nineteen skeletons altogether. Those of the women were covered with thin gold disks which, as we know from the paintings, were originally sewn to their dresses. Gold bracelets, signets, and diadems were also found with the women.

Beautiful pottery, breastplates, and beads filled the graves of the men, as they did those of the women. There were also bronze swords with pommels of gold and ivory, bronze mirrors with handles of ivory, and various objects made of rock crystal, faïence (a colorful glazed earthenware), and electrum (an alloy of gold and silver). Especially interesting are the gold death masks, which reveal the dignity and character of strong men who had constantly to defend their civilization against invasions from the north. Their proudest weapon was a bronze dagger, down the middle of which was inlaid a strip of dark gold. Inlaid on the dark gold — in silver, light gold, and niello (the dark metallic alloy of sulfur with silver or copper) — were scenes from life. These included scenes such as armed men hunting lions. On November 28, 1876, Schliemann triumphantly and enthusiastically telegraphed King George of Greece announcing the discovery of the graves of the king's royal ancestors.

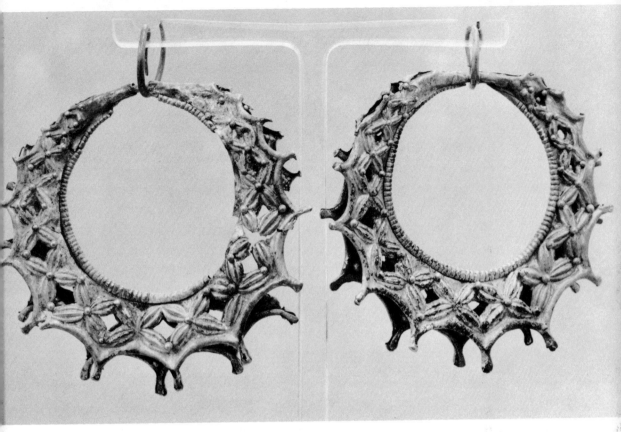

Gold earrings from Mycenae. Beautiful jewelry was worn by both men and women.

HIRMER FOTOARCHIV

An armlet from Mycenae.   HIRMER FOTOARCHIV

Most famous of all the Mycenaean metalwork are two gold cups found in a tomb as far away as Vaphio, near Sparta. The embossed scenes on the cups show the capture and taming of wild bulls. But Mycenaean influences spread farther even than Sparta. Mycenaean boats, propelled by oars and sails, went to Egypt, Italy, and other distant lands. By 1300 B.C., after having humbled Knossos, Mycenae reached the zenith of its power.

The Mycenaeans and their Citadel

IT WAS in 1300 B.C. that Mycenae's ruling dynasty decided to surround the citadel with an immense wall, twenty-three feet thick and sixty feet high. The blocks of stone are so huge that the classical Greeks imagined that only Homer's one-eyed giants, the Cyclopes, could have built them; for that reason, we ourselves call such walls "Cyclopean."

The main entrance through this wall was by means of the famous Lion Gate. On either side of the gateway, which was originally closed by double doors, stand the upright doorjambs. Stretching from the top of one jamb to the top of the other is the stone lintel. The Mycenaean architects, who of course had tremendous engineering skill, believed that if they continued the layers, or courses, of the fortification wall straight across the lintel, the weight would break it. Instead, therefore, they made an arch over the lintel in such a way that the weight would come down on the jambs and thus directly to the ground. This is how they did it.

The Mycenaeans did not know the keystone arch, in which a wedge-shaped stone is placed in the center of the arch to hold the structure together. They did, however, have the corbel. With a corbel arch, each course of stones projects slightly beyond the course below. This is done on both sides of the empty area and is repeated with each course until the empty space narrows to the point where the two sides touch. Now there is an empty triangular area between the lintel and the arch. Archeologists call this the "relieving triangle" because it relieves the lintel of weight.

Naturally, the relieving triangle had to be filled; otherwise an enemy might creep through it. Accordingly, the builders of the pal-

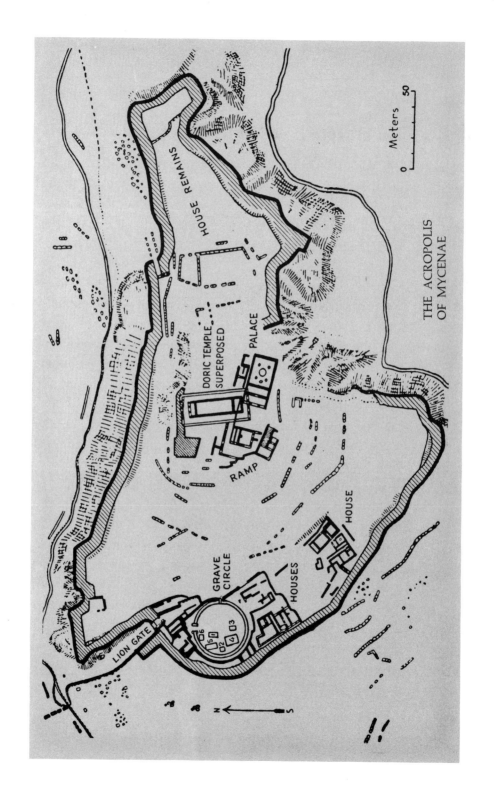

THE ACROPOLIS
OF MYCENAE

HOUSE REMAINS

DORIC TEMPLE
SUPERPOSED

PALACE

RAMP

GRAVE
CIRCLE

HOUSES

HOUSE

LION GATE

N

S

Meters

0   50

The heavy, Cyclopean fortification wall at Mycenae, originally 60 feet high and 23 feet thick; 1300 B.C. The entrance is capped by the famous sculptured relief of lions.

PHOTO BY PHILIP GENDREAU

ace placed in the empty space a much lighter block of stone, carved with representations of lions on either side of a column, above which there appear the beams of a roof. Column and beams represent the palace, while the lions signify the great power of the king who stands ready to protect his people.

The common people of Mycenae came inside the citadel only in times of danger. They lived ordinarily in settlements scattered along the nearby hills. The typical Mycenaean house was deep, narrow, and rectangular, and had a flat roof. In front was a porch, with wooden columns on stone bases; a door led into the main room. Here was the hearth, where the family ate, relaxed, and slept. A room to the rear, used for storage, completed the small dwelling. Most of the people spent their time either in cultivating grain (wheat, barley, oats, rye), lentils, fruit and olive trees, and grapes; or in looking after the animals — oxen, sheep, pigs, goats — which provided them with meat, clothing, and fat for fuel.

Not everyone, however, needed to be a farmer or shepherd. Some men made pottery or tools — plows, kettles, knives, etc. Others made textiles. The Mycenaeans made excellent clothing, baskets, and fishnets because they knew how to spin and weave flax and wool.

Some clay tablets inscribed in the Mycenaean script have recently been found and translated. They speak of men engaged in various trades and professions, as they are in advanced civilizations today. The tablets mention smiths, cooks, physicians, masons, carpenters, bowmakers, tailors, bath attendants, woodcutters, landowning citizens, and kings. There are also references to the priests who performed sacrifices to such gods as Poseidon, Athena, Apollo, and others. Minoan characteristics, such as the worship of the Great Mother goddess, also appear in the Mycenaean religion.

The king, his family, and retainers lived within the citadel itself. The palace was on the very top of the hill, with a spacious court and Hall of State, a throne room, bedrooms, a bathroom, and a shrine. An earthquake has damaged the palace severely.

The Mycenaean wall paintings are gay and colorful, and are likely to emphasize such things as battle scenes and boar hunts. Despite all the cultural influences from Crete, the Mycenaeans could not quite grasp the unadulterated and sheer sense of beauty possessed by the Minoans. Perhaps this was inevitable, because the Cyclopean wall of Mycenae proves that a vigorous life of warfare was often the order of the day.

Mycenae's Great Beehive Tombs

THE COMMON PEOPLE of Mycenae had very simple graves, just holes scooped out of the ground. If the survivors could afford it, they placed stones at either end of the dead man, with a slab of stone across the top of the body. They were almost certain to bury a few objects, such as pots, with him.

Grand as were the rock-cut chambers of the nobles, nothing can match the architectural magnificence of the tombs of Mycenae's kings. These are usually spoken of as beehive tombs, because they look strangely like beehives. There are nine of these tombs at Mycenae, and about forty elsewhere in Greece.

The biggest and most wonderful of all these tombs was the so-called Treasury of Atreus at Mycenae. It was probably built by the king who put the Cyclopean wall around the citadel. It is easy to understand why a beehive tomb should be called a "treasury." Those that have not already been robbed are full of gold and bronze utensils, weapons, and other objects. The Treasury of Atreus was named by Schliemann after the father of Agamemnon, leader of the Greeks against Troy.

The tombs of the nobles and the kings resemble each other in that both have *dromos* and burial chambers. The *dromos* of the Treasury of Atreus is 115 feet long and 20 feet wide. Instead of leaving its sides of earth exposed, the architect lined them with blocks of stone.

At the end of the *dromos* is the doorway, 18 feet high, and capped by two tremendous lintel blocks, the inner one weighing 120 tons. Slaves probably pushed it into place by means of rollers and a ramp. Columns of green stone stood on either side of the doorway. Above the lintel is the familiar relieving triangle, now empty, but originally filled by red porphyry slabs carved with spirals. Lord Elgin brought these slabs and one of the stone columns to London early in the last century and gave them to the British Museum.

Unlike the rock-cut tombs of the nobles, whose chambers were dug out from the doorway, the chamber of a beehive tomb was excavated from above. The people who built the Treasury of Atreus dug a huge hole from the top of the hill, forty-four feet deep and

From a beehive at Vaphio, near Sparta, came two gold cups, with embossed scenes. Here we see a strong bull, against the background of a formalized tree, tethered by a Mycenaean Greek. The handles of the cups are riveted on. About 1500 B. C.

HIRMER FOTOARCHIV

forty-eight feet in diameter. They then lined the circular hole with stone blocks, each course projecting slightly beyond the course below. Little by little, as the courses were laid, the diameter became less, until finally the corbel system had done its work and the whole chamber was arched over. Sacrifices, dances, and other ceremonies in honor of the dead were performed in this chamber. The dead were buried in a small room to one side.

This gold cup from Vaphio shows the taming of the bulls after their capture. The metal work of Mycenaean Greece ranks with the highest in the history of art.

The Treasury of Atreus was being used as a sheepfold when Schliemann first came to Mycenae; at some moment in the dim past it had been robbed of its contents. Nevertheless, it stands as one of the architectural wonders of the world, quietly awe-inspiring and magnificently alone in all its splendor, facing out from its hillside across the Argive Plain to the sea. It represents the Greek genius as surely as does the Athenian Parthenon, built some nine centuries later.

56

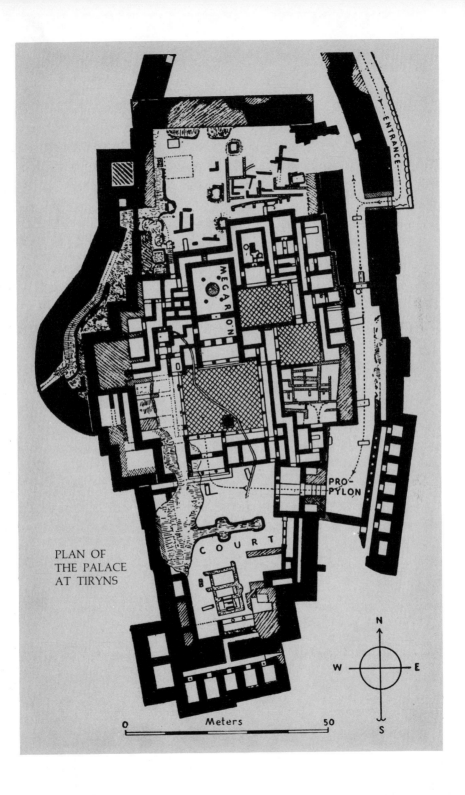

ENTRANCE

MEGARON

PRO-
PYLON

COURT

PLAN OF
THE PALACE
AT TIRYNS

N
W   E
S

0   Meters   50

Tiryns

ALTHOUGH the Mycenaean kings were so powerful that they became the leaders of Greece, other kings and princes were also rich and mighty, as their royal residences testify. One such place is Tiryns, a magnificently grim citadel between Mycenae and the sea, with a palace that is fortunately well preserved.

Like Mycenae, Tiryns has a Cyclopean wall made of huge blocks; in places it is fifty-seven feet thick. The entrance ramp is particularly interesting, because it leads up to the gateway in such a way that your right side is next to the wall. Now, if you were an enemy coming up that ramp with defenders shooting at you from the walls, you would have to shift your shield to your right arm to protect yourself and then you could not fight back (most people then, as now, being right-handed).

Even if you forced the gateway, it would not help you much, because straight ahead of you is another immense wall, with other gates to left and right. It was probably impossible to capture these citadels, except by starvation or treachery, since siege engines did not exist for knocking down the walls. At two points within the walls of Tiryns are storage chambers, so we can be sure the king was always ready to stand off invaders; there was also a spring, as there was at Mycenae.

A friendly visitor to Tiryns would walk through monumental gateways and finally into a paved court, which contains an altar for sacrifices to the gods. The court is surrounded by columns, beyond which are various rooms of the palace. The chief area is the Hall of State (Megaron), which is merely an elaboration of the ordinary private house. Its porch, with two columns, had a bench of alabaster (a mineral of white, translucent crystals) inlaid with blue paste.

Three doorways lead into a vestibule, from which you enter the main room.

The main room has a raised seat, or dais, which served as the throne. The floor is made of stucco, inlaid with red and yellow squares in various patterns and with blue squares decorated by octopuses and dolphins. In the center is the hearth, around which stood four columns: these held up the ceiling, which had a hole in it to let out the smoke.

Here in the main room the king and his intimate friends would listen to professional poets and singers known as bards, who traveled from town to town, singing about the deeds of local heroes. Thus there grew up during the Bronze Age a whole body of song and poetry — epic sagas, which ultimately Homer developed and wove into his immortal poems.

The palace at Tiryns had many other formal rooms, bedrooms, bathrooms, courts, and corridors. In places it was two stories high, with a flat roof. The colorful paintings, as was typical of the day, are imbued with a military spirit; there are also hunting scenes, with men driving off in their chariots, accompanied by slaves and dogs, to kill a boar; and still other paintings show beautiful women wearing richly adorned dresses.

Bronze Age Greece represented a baronial type of life, with the few rich enjoying their estates and lording it over the many poor. But it was not destined to last forever.

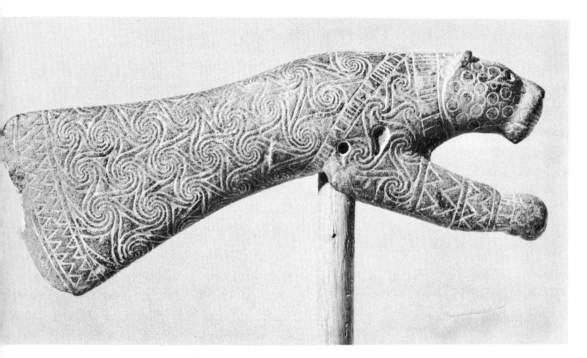

A mace-head in the form of a vigorous leopard. It is made of gray schist (a crystalline stone) and was used as a battle-ax. From the palace of Mallia.

HIRMER FOTOARCHIV

The Linear B Tables

PROFESSOR Carl W. Blegen of the University of Cincinnati, who is probably America's greatest archeologist, has excavated at Pylos, in southwestern Greece, the palace that once belonged to King Nestor. According to Homer, Nestor accompanied Agamemnon to Troy.

In the years just before and after World War II, Blegen found in his excavations more than one thousand tablets, inscribed in a strange syllabic script; others like them have been dug up at Mycenae and elsewhere. For the sake of convenience, these tablets are called Linear B (to differentiate them from the Linear A tablets found by Evans at Knossos).

The secret of the Linear B was cracked by a young English architect in 1952 — Michael Ventris by name. Not long afterward, he was killed in a motor accident. Ventris will live in history with all those people who have succeeded in deciphering strange writings, men such as Champollion, whose work on the Rosetta Stone has recovered the ancient Egyptian language for us.

The most important fact discovered by Ventris is that the language of the Linear B tablets — not the strange script itself — is Greek. That is why we now know that the people who began coming into Greece around 2000 B.C. were Greeks; and the civilization they built at Mycenae and other places was Greek.

A terribly sad and anxious tone is struck by the latest of the tablets found by Blegen, those from around 1100 B.C. The writer speaks of a crisis brewing, of an enemy somewhere in the distance. Feverish military preparations have begun. The women and children, according to the tablets, are gathered together in two places. A list is drawn up of the boys who can row; apparently the population was going to flee to islands. There is the reassuring note that enough bronze has been brought together to make several hundred thousand arrowheads. Finally, we read, the troops have been equipped and mobilized; sentries have been placed at strategic points to watch for the enemy.

That is all. Nothing but silence follows. The enemy came, and that was the end of Mycenae and the Bronze Age.

61

In the Palace of King Nestor at Pylos, Carl W. Blegen excavated 1,000 clay tablets inscribed in a strange syllabic script. called for convenience Linear B. This proved, for the first time, that the Mycenaean mainland possessed writing. Next, Michael Ventris by cracking the secret of the script showed that its language is Greek. This proved, for the first time, that these people and their civilization were Greek (the most dramatic archeological discovery of the last half century). A chief aid to Ventris was the tablet here illustrated. The top line has pictures of three-legged

vases; the next two lines, pictures of four-handled, three-handled, and no-handled vases. Ventris experimented by assuming that a sign near the three-legged and three-handled vases stood for the Greek word "tri" (three); one "guess" led to another — for example, that three oft-repeated signs stood for KO-NO-SO (Knossos) — until finally a regular vocabulary was established. It will be noted that our tablet is an inventory and that the final picture lists only one no-handled vase.

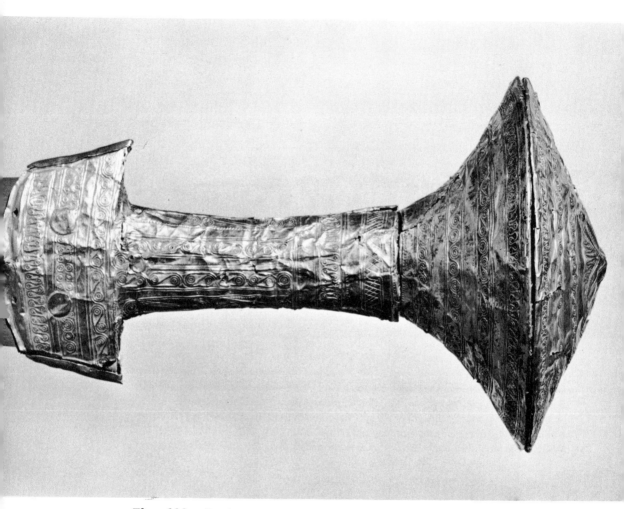

The gold handle of a ceremonial sword belonging to a proud Mycenaean.

HIRMER FOTOARCHIV

The End of The Bronze Age

THE DECLINE of Mycenae and its Bronze Age world must be intimately associated with its increasing wealth. Trade demanded more and more products, rapidly turned out; art became an industry. The people themselves began to prefer the showy and flamboyant; simplicity gave way to stylization and the constant repetition of themes in art. Imitation killed originality. All history proves that when this happens, the human spirit begins to wither, and intellectual inquiry is dead.

On the other hand, history shows — as with the Incas or the Roman Empire — that a declining society can totter along for an almost indefinite period. Some violent blow is needed to bring it finally to an end.

In the case of Mycenae and its society, the end came about 1100 B.C. with the arrival from the north of the Dorians. The Dorians were a branch of the Greek people, invading a land that had been Greek since 2000 B.C. They were rough and vigorous. Organized in tribes under their chieftains, they fell upon an urbanized world that had long been accustomed to the ways of civilization. Above all, perhaps, they possessed iron — a metal superior to bronze — and the better weapons in the hands of the warlike won out.

The great palaces of the Mycenaeans went up in smoke — a catastrophe which, at least for us, was a blessing, because it baked and thereby preserved the inscribed clay tablets. The kings lost their heads, of course, but most people lived on. Life was simpler for three centuries or so. And then, once again, the Greeks surged forward and created the great classical civilization that has inspired men ever since.

65

The Legacy
of Ancient Crete and Mycenae

THE OVERWHELMING fact about the Minoans of Crete is their sense
of beauty. No one has yet explained satisfactorily why some people
seem to be more gifted intellectually and artistically than others.
Even more extraordinary, in a certain way, is the fact that the
Minoans began, as it were, from scratch. Most other people in history have had past achievements on which to draw, but the Minoans
were at the beginning of things, so far as their own world was con-
cerned. They did receive some influences from the more ancient
civilizations of Egypt and Mesopotamia, but these were unimportant,
and the Minoans gave as much as they received.

A great monument, such as the palace of Minos at Knossos, is
magnificent in its entirety, and in its various parts as well. Let us
skip over the large wall paintings — whether of partridges, or a cup-
bearer, or the priest king himself — and consider a fragment small
enough to hold in our hand. It is simply a piece of plaster, on which
the artist painted while it was still wet so that the painting soaked
right into the plaster. The colorful fragment may show nothing more
than a reed blowing in the wind or the head of a monkey, but it has
been executed with love and understanding and skill. Exquisite
beauty is the result.

The major art of wall decoration influenced the pottery. Some of
the vases have been manufactured so well, and have been made so
thin, that archeologists call their manufacture "egg shell." The decoration is an exciting combination of many colors, called polychromy,
with abstract or naturalistic designs.

A lead figure of a typically slim Mycenaean Greek, with a loincloth around his narrow waist.

When we understand these and the other achievements of the Minoans, we are in a better position to decide for ourselves what our own standards of taste should be. A knowledge of history both inspires us to copy and improve on the past, and also warns us to avoid certain things.

The gifted Mycenaeans, for example, in search of ever wider markets, eventually turned art into industry. Original thinking dried up. Then, too, the Mycenaeans lacked the profound peace which nurtured the wonderful flowering of the human spirit in Crete. To be sure, they took much from the Minoans and added it to their own civilization, but they also had to spend a good deal of their time and energy fighting off waves of northern invaders.

These invaders were Greeks, as the Mycenaeans themselves were, and they had been arriving in their historic homeland ever since 2000 B.C. At first, they came in small enough numbers to be absorbed, but the Dorian Greeks came in such large bands around 1100 B.C. that the Age of Crete and Mycenae ended. The Bronze Age yielded to the Iron Age.

Much of the past carried over into the new period — town life, for instance. And it is fair to guess that the classical Greeks inherited, at least partially, from their predecessors their love of beauty and their love of sports (the one illustrated by the Athenian Parthenon, the other by the Olympic Games). Accordingly Crete and Mycenae are important in their own right and also for their contributions to classical Greece. The distinguished modern historian, Arnold Toynbee, has called Greek civilization "the finest flower of the species that has ever yet come to bloom."

A beautiful rhyton of silver and gold, from the Grave Circle of Mycenae's citadel.

The invasion of the Dorian Greeks was violent enough to end detailed knowledge of the preceding period. Instead of historical research, there grew up a mass of legends concerning a supposedly heroic past; much of it was added to tales that had actually developed during the Bronze Age. The result of this was that about 800 B.C. one of the greatest poets of all time — Homer — was able to weave together his two epics, the *Iliad* and the *Odyssey*.

The Homeric poems were long the chief "evidence" that men had about Greece in the Bronze Age. It may be terrifying to reflect that all true knowledge of a great civilization can disappear for three thousand years. But it is also downright exciting to observe how scholars in our own day have been able to recover it.

Index